The Missions: California's Heritage

MISSION
LA PURÍSIMA CONCEPCIÓN

by

Mary Null Boulé

Merryant Publishers, Inc.
10920 Palisades Ave. SW
Vashon, WA 98070
206-463-3879
Fax 206-463-1604
http://merryantpublishers.com/

With special thanks to Msgr. Francis J. Weber, Archivist of the Los Angeles Catholic Diocese for his encouragement and expertise in developing this series.

This series is dedicated to my sister, Nancy Null Kenyon, whose editing skills and support were so freely given.

ISBN: 978-1-877599-10-1

Father Junípero Serra

INTRODUCTION

Building of a mission church involved everyone in the mission community. Priests were engineers and architects; Native Americans did the construction. Mission Indian in front is pouring adobe mix into a brick form. Bricks were then dried in the sun.

FATHER SERRA AND THE MISSIONS: AN INTRODUCTION

The year was 1769. On the east coast of what would soon become the United States, the thirteen original colonies were making ready to break away from England. On the west coast of our continent, however, there could be found only untamed land inhabited by Native Americans, or Indians. Although European explorers had sailed up and down the coast in their ships, no one but American Indians had explored the length of this land on foot . . . until now.

To this wild, beautiful country came a group of adventurous men from New Spain, as Mexico was then called. They were following the orders of their king, King Charles III of Spain.

One of the men was a Spanish missionary named Fray Junípero Serra. He had been given a tremendous job; especially since he was fifty-six years old, an old man in those days. King Charles III had ordered mission settlements to be built along the coast of Alta (Upper) California and it was Fr. Serra's task to carry out the king's wishes.

Father Serra had been born in the tiny village of Petra

on the island of Mallorca, Spain. He had done such an excellent job of teaching and working with the Indians in Mexican missions, the governor of New Spain had suggested to the king that Fr. Serra do the same with the Indians of Alta California. Hard-working Fray Serra was helped by Don Gaspár de Portolá, newly chosen governor of Alta California, and two other Franciscan priests who had grown up with Fr. Serra in Mallorca, Father Fermin Lasuén and Father Francisco Palóu.

There were several reasons why men had been told to build settlements along the coast of this unexplored country. First, missions would help keep the land as Spanish territory. Spain wanted to be sure the rest of the world knew it owned this rich land. Second, missions were to be built near harbors so towns would grow there. Ships from other countries could then stop to trade with the Spaniards, but these travelers could not try to claim the land for themselves. Third, missions were a good way to turn Indians into Christian, hard-working people.

It would be nice if we could write here that everything went well; that twenty-one missions immediately sprang up along the coast. Unfortunately, all did not go well. It would take fifty-four years to build all the California missions. During those fifty-four years many people died from Indian attacks, sickness, and starvation. Earthquakes and fires constantly ruined mission buildings, which then had to be built all over again. Fr. Serra calmly overcame each problem as it happened, as did those priests who followed him.

When a weary Fray Serra finally died in 1784, he had founded nine missions from San Diego to Monterey and had arranged the building of many more. Fr. Lasuén continued Fr. Serra's work, adding eight more missions to the California mission chain. The remaining four missions were founded in later years.

Originally, plans had been to place missions a hard day's walk from each other. Many of them were really quite far apart. Travelers truly struggled to go from one mission to another along the 650 miles of walking road known as El Camino Real, The Royal Highway. Today keen eyes will sometimes see tall, curved poles with bells hanging from them sitting by the side of streets and highways. These bell poles are marking a part of the old El Camino Real.

At first Spanish soldiers were put in charge of the towns which grew up near each mission. The priests were told to handle only the mission and its properties. It did not take long to realize the soldiers were not kind and gentle leaders. Many were uneducated and did not have the understanding they should have had in dealing with people. So the padres came to be in charge of not only the mission, but of the townspeople and even of the soldiers.

The first missions at San Diego and Monterey were built near the ocean where ships could bring them needed supplies. After early missions began to grow their own food and care for themselves, later mission compounds were built farther away from the coast. What one mission did well, such as leatherworking, candlemaking, or raising cattle, was shared with other missions. As a result, missions became somewhat specialized in certain products.

Although mission buildings looked different from mission to mission, most were built from one basic plan. Usually a compound was constructed as a large, four-sided building with an inner patio in the center. The outside of the quadrangle had only one or two doors, which were locked at night to protect the mission. A church usually sat at one corner of the quadrangle and was always the tallest and largest part of the mission compound.

Facing the inner patio were rooms for the two priests living there, workshops, a kitchen, storage rooms for grain and food, and the mission office. Rooms along the back of the quadrangle often served as home to the unmarried Indian women who worked in the kitchen. The rest of the Indians lived just outside the walls of the mission in their own village.

Beyond the mission wall and next to the church was a cemetery. Today you can still see many of the original headstones of those who died while living and working at the mission. Also outside the walls were larger workshops, a reservoir holding water used at the mission, and orchards containing fruit trees. Huge fields surrounded each mission where crops grew and livestock such as sheep, cattle, and horses grazed.

It took a great deal of time for some Indian tribes to understand the new way of life a mission offered, even though the

Native Americans always had food and shelter when they became mission Indians. Each morning all Indians were awakened at sunrise by a church bell calling them to church. Breakfast followed church . . . and then work. The women spun thread and made clothes, as well as cooked meals. Men and older boys worked in workshops or fields and constructed buildings. Meanwhile the Indian children went to school, where the padres taught them. After a noon meal there was a two hour rest before work began again. After dinner the Indians sang, played, or danced. This way of life was an enormous change from the less organized Indian life before the missionaries arrived. Many tribes accepted the change, some had more trouble getting used to a regular schedule, some tribes never became a part of mission life.

Water was all-important to the missions. It was needed to irrigate crops and to provide for the mission people and animals. Priests designed and engineered magnificent irrigation systems at most of the missions. All building of aqueducts and reservoirs of these systems was done by the mission Indians.

With all the organized hard work, the missions did very well. They grew and became strong. Excellent vineyards gave wine for the priests to use and to sell. Mission fields produced large grain crops of wheat and corn, and vast grazing land developed huge herds of cattle and sheep. Mission life was successful for over fifty years.

When Mexico broke away from Spain, it found it did not have enough money to support the California missions, as Spain had been doing. So in 1834, Mexico enforced the secularization law which their government had decreed several years earlier. This law stated missions were to be taken away from the missionaries and given to the Indians. The law said that if an Indian did not want the land or buildings, the property was to be sold to anyone who wished to buy it.

It is true the missions had become quite large and powerful. And as shocked as the padres were to learn of the secularization law, they also knew the missions had originally been planned as temporary, or short term projects. The priests had been sure their Indians would be well-trained enough to run the missions by themselves when the time came to move to other unsettled lands. In fact, however, even after fifty years the California Indians were still not ready to handle the huge missions.

Since the Indians did not wish to continue the missions, the buildings and land were sold, the Indians not even waiting for money or, in some cases, receiving money for the sale.

Sad times lay ahead. Many Indians went back to the old way of life. Some Indians stayed on as servants to the new owners and often these owners were not good to them. Mission buildings were used for everything from stores and saloons to animal barns. In one mission the church became a barracks for the army. A balcony was built for soldiers with their horses stabled in the altar area. Rats ate the stored grain and beautiful church robes. Furniture and objects left by the padres were stolen. People even stole the mission building roof tiles, which then caused the adobe brick walls to melt from rain. Earthquakes finished off many buildings.

Shortly after California became a part of the United States in the mid-1850s, our government returned all mission buildings to the Catholic Church. By this time most of them were in terrible condition. Since the priests needed only the church itself and a few rooms to live in, the other rooms of the mission were rented to anyone who needed them. Strange uses were found in some cases. In the San Fernando Mission, for example, there was once a pig farm in the patio area.

Tourists finally began to notice the mission ruins in the early 1900s. Groups of interested people got together to see if the missions could be restored. Some missions had been "modernized" by this time, unfortunately, but within the last thirty years historians have found enough pictures, drawings, and written descriptions to rebuild or restore most of the missions to their original appearances.

The restoration of all twenty-one missions is a splendid way to preserve our California heritage. It is the hope of many Californians that this dream of restoration can become a reality in the near future.

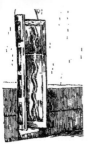

LA PURÍSIMA CONCEPCIÓN

I. THE MISSION TODAY

La Purísima Concepción is the truest form of old mission life to be found in California. The mission has been almost completely restored. All that is missing from the present day mission are the Franciscan missionary padres and the mission Indians of long ago.

La Purísima is the only mission built in a straight line instead of the usual quadrangle. It is at the base of a hill in a small canyon named La Canada de los Berros (Canyon of Watercress). It is wonderfully away from modern towns and people. The closest town is Lompoc, and it is at least four miles away.

Walking towards the mission on a dirt path which crosses a huge meadow, one sees fenced fields with burros, goats, sheep, and cattle grazing, just as in mission days. The most exciting moment of the walk is crossing a dirt trail that is actually a part of the original El Camino Real!

The first mission area you come to is the plain, walled cemetery. A large wooden cross had been placed there to honor all those who are buried there. The cemetery has no flowers, trees, or grass. The front wall of the cemetery contains the companario, or bell wall. Original bells hanging there come from Lima, Peru. They were made especially for La Purísima in 1817-1818. During the time the mission was left alone, other missions cared for the bells. They were brought back to La Purísima when restoration began in the 1930s.

Next to the cemetery is the great long church. It has been well-restored. The adobe walls are four feet thick, and the roof is tile. Although the church is very narrow, in mission days it could easily hold 1,000 Indians for church services. The outside of the church has been painted an almost white color with reddish-brown along the foundation.

Inside the church is a carefully restored sanctuary with an altar, a fresco-style reredos and an old Sanctus bell wheel. The pulpit sits high up on the right wall. Father Mariano Payeras, who came to La Purísima in 1804, and remained there until his death in 1823, is buried beneath the altar. There are no pews, but benches have been placed along the side walls of the huge room. Oil paintings of the Stations of the Cross hang on the walls. The floor is of uneven tile, just as in mission times. The main entrance to the church is on the side wall, near the path that was El Camino Real. San Gabriel Mission had its entrance on the side wall for the same reason, to be near the El Camino Real. Sadly, this building at La Purísima, however, is not still used as a church, like San Gabriel is.

Next to the church is the long residence building containing soldiers' quarters and Indian workshops. Most of the many rooms open to a back patio as well as to the front corridor. Actually, corridors run along both the front and back of this building. Each room has been furnished with furniture and tools exactly like those used by the people of mission days. These rooms are so complete, one expects to see mission soldiers or Indians walk in at any moment.

The third long building in the row of restored buildings is the padres' residence. It was built with a massive stone buttress on one end to keep it strong during earthquakes. Besides the priests' rooms, a library, offices, guest rooms, the wine cellar, and the mission store, there is also a large chapel that was used for church services after the main church became unsafe in 1830.

Behind the padres' building and soldiers' quarters are the group kitchen-grist mill, and the pottery shop. A blacksmith's shop, a springhouse where water was stored, and a girls' dormitory have also been restored on original foundations on the patio side of the mission buildings. Just behind the cemetery are large furnaces where animal fat was boiled for the tallow used in soap and candle-making.

The visitor center and museum have been placed in what were old infirmary buildings. It was here sick Native Americans were cared for by mission priests.

These mission grounds are an historical state park and so are well-cared for by the California State Department of Parks and Recreation. What makes this restoration so interesting is that all mission life is here to see. As a matter of fact, Mission La Purisima Concepción is the largest and most complete restoration done in our Historic West.

II. HISTORY OF THE MISSION

La Purisima Concepción de Maria Santisima was the official name given to Mission La Purisima by Father Fermin Lasuén when he founded the mission on December 8, 1787. The name translates from Spanish to mean "The Immaculate Conception of Mary the Most Pure." Fr. Lasuén, who took over as president of the California Missions at the death of Father Junipero Serra, was following orders Fr. Serra had left: That there be three missions in this area to take care of the many tribes of Chumash Indians living nearby.

The priests had to wait until spring of the next year to begin the buildings of the mission, however, for the winter was too rainy that first year. Then the mission grew rapidly and by 1791 the first mission buildings were completed and the mission was already a busy place. In 1802, the original huts had been replaced by ones of adobe brick with tile roofs. It was at this time that European traders began to ask the Chumash Indians to hunt animals for them. The traders especially wanted sea otter skins to sell in Europe. They so bothered the Chumash Island Indians, that most of the natives left their Channel Islands and moved to the mainland, near La Purisima. This made the mission grow even faster.

Father Mariano Payeras arrived in 1804. He became one of the most successful of all the mission priests, staying at La Purisima until his death nineteen years later. Four of those years he was Father-president of the whole mission chain: but he continued to stay at La Purisima, taking care of his duties there instead of moving to Mission Carmel, where the "presidentes" usually lived.

Fr. Payeras realized at once there was not enough water to grow all the food needed for such a fast-growing mission. He designed an irrigation system himself, and the crops immediately improved. The mission became well-known for its soap, candles, wool, and leather goods. At the time Fr. Payeras arrived there were 1,522 Indians living at the mission. Suddenly the Native Americans began to die in great numbers.

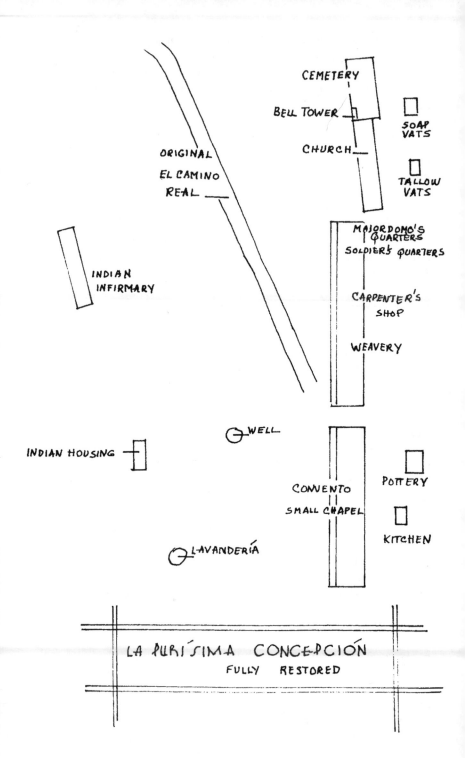

CEMETERY

BELL TOWER

ORIGINAL
EL CAMINO
REAL

CHURCH

SOAP VATS

TALLOW VATS

INDIAN INFIRMARY

MAJORDOMO'S QUARTERS

SOLDIERS QUARTERS

CARPENTER'S SHOP

WEAVERY

WELL

INDIAN HOUSING

POTTERY

CONVENTO

SMALL CHAPEL

KITCHEN

LAVANDERÍA

LA PURÍSIMA CONCEPCIÓN
FULLY RESTORED

They simply could not fight off the white man's diseases such as smallpox and measles. Within three years, 1804-1807, nearly 500 Indians were buried at La Purisima. The crops continued to grow larger, but the mission population grew smaller every year.

As if the dying Indians were not bad enough, terrible earthquakes hit the mission in December of 1812. Not only were the mission buildings destroyed, but huge cracks in the earth opened up near the mission site. Drenching rains then fell on mission ruins for several weeks. It was too much. The Indians refused to go back to the mission site. Father Payeras decided to move the whole mission four miles northeast, to Canyon of Watercress, where it stands today.

The mission was rebuilt, this time with much stronger buildings. Although Fr. Payeras became Father-presidente of all the missions in 1815, he continued to be in charge of rebuilding La Purisima. The church, residence building, and priests' residence were completed by 1818, and except for the bell wall finished in 1821, no other large buildings were ever constructed after 1818.

There were many reasons all building stopped at La Purisima, all the missions, for that matter. Mexico had been trying to break away from Spain's rule for a long time. In 1810 there was a revolution in Mexico which caused Spain to stop sending money to California to take care of the soldiers and priests there. Worse yet, the revolution stopped the money missions were just beginning to make by selling hemp, or rope, to other countries.

Soldiers had to turn to the missions for food, clothing, and Indian helpers. The soldiers were not at all kind to the natives. Their anger grew until, in 1824, an Indian revolt at Mission Santa Inés spread to La Purisima. Here the Indians actually built the mission into a fort with walls of wooden stakes. They moved two small cannons into place by the wall. These cannons were the kind used only by priests to make noise on special feast days at the church. Mission Indians actually controlled the mission this way for nearly a month, but when the soldiers finally arrived to attack the mission, it took only two and one-half hours for the Indians to give in. Through all the trouble, the priests remained at the mission.

In 1826, spring water bubbled up from the ground right under the main church. It damaged church walls so badly that priests could no longer use it for church services. The priests' own smaller chapel was made larger and used as the main church from that time on.

In 1834, secularization became law. Mayordomos were sent from Mexico to take over management of the missions. Some of these men proved to be greedy, and in only six months over half the wealth of La Purisima was nowhere to be found. The two Spanish priests who had been living at the mission moved to Mission Santa Inés to live. After that priests came back to the mission only to baptize or to perform funerals.

The mission began to fall apart, and by 1844 only 200 Indians and the soldiers' residence building remained. The mission was sold the first time that year, for only $1,100. The new owners lived in the residence building, as did other owners through the years. Often the building housed sheep or cattle and once there was even a saloon in one part of it. In 1880 a fire burned part of the roof. Finally, in 1904, all roof tiles were taken down so they would not fall on anyone. The adobe walls began to dissolve immediately after the tiles were removed.

By the time restoration began in 1934, only nine of the original eighteen columns outside the residence building and some piles of melted adobe were left of La Purisima Concepción. When it was learned the government Civilian Conservation Corps (CCC) would restore La Purisima if enough land could be given back to make the mission into an historical monument, the Catholic Church and Union Oil Company donated the needed land. Thus began the most complete restoration ever tried.

Two hundred men of the CCC took seven years to rebuild the mission exactly as it used to be. This time the adobe brick was reinforced with hidden steel girders. Each brick was made in the same way the Indians had made them originally. Every building foundation was carefully uncovered and objects found while digging were gently removed and saved.

Dedication Day of the restored mission was almost 154 years to the day of the founding date of La Purisima Concepción. The date was December 7, 1941, the first day of World War II for the United States.

Interior of restored church. Long and narrow, it could hold as many as a thousand Indians at one time. The grave of Fr. Payeras is buried beneath the altar. Note "river of life" pattern on the front entrance doors. El Camino Real leading to other missions was outside these doors.

Animal hides hang on racks in field in front of the long, straight mission. Cemetery is behind wall to the left; church is to the right of bell tower; soldiers' quarters is on far right; priests' quarters containing the small chapel used for many years as the church is beyond soldiers' building.

OUTLINE OF LA PURÍSIMA

I. **The mission today**
   A. Completely restored
   B. Shape of mission different
   C. Location
      1. La Canada de los Berros
      2. Near Lompoc
   D. El Camino Real
   E. Cemetery description
   F. Campanario and bell history
   G. Exterior of church
      1. Adobe walls
      2. Tile roof
      3. Color and trim
   H. Church interior
      1. Sanctuary
         a. Altar, reredos, and bell wheel
      2. Pulpit
      3. Fr. Payeras buried there
      4. Benches, but no pews
      5. Stations of the Cross paintings
      6. Flooring
      7. Chandeliers and ceiling
      8. Side door entrance
   I. Residence building
      1. Soldiers' quarters
      2. Workshops
   J. Padres' residence building
      1. Massive buttress
      2. Kinds of rooms
      3. Priests' chapel
   K. Smaller buildings on patio side of residences
      1. Group kitchen-grist mill, etc.
   L. Tallow furnaces
   M. Visitor's center and museum
      1. Old infirmary buildings
   N. Care of mission by Park Department

Outline continued next page

II. History of Mission

A. Founding
   1. Founder and date
B. Delay in starting mission
C. 1791
   1. Still original small buildings
   2. Thriving mission
D. New adobe buildings in 1802
E. Father Payeras
   1. Traders bother island Indians
   2. Mission grows
   3. New water system
F. Products of mission
G. Indian sickness
   1. Population shrinks
   2. Crops grow larger
H. 1812 earthquakes
I. New site (present site)
J. Mexican - Spanish revolution
   1. Mission money stopped
   2. Soldiers misuse missions and Indians
K. Indian revolts
   1. La Purisima held by Indians
L. Main church abandoned
   1. Small priests' chapel enlarged
M. Secularization
   1. Mayordomos
   2. Missions stripped of valuables
   3. Priests leave la Purisima
N. Mission sold
   1. Many uses of mission
O. Fire ruins roof
   1. Roof removed
   2. Mission collapses
P. Restoration begins
   1. CCC
   2. Exact restoration takes seven years
   3. Dedication Day on Pearl Harbor Day

GLOSSARY

BUTTRESS: a large mass of stone or wood used to strengthen buildings

CAMPANARIO: a wall which holds bells

CLOISTER: an enclosed area; a word often used instead of convento

CONVENTO: mission building where priests lived

CORRIDOR: covered, outside hallway found at most missions

EL CAMINO REAL: highway between missions; also known as The King's Highway

FACADE: front wall of a building

FONT: large, often decorated bowl containing Holy Water for baptizing people

FOUNDATION: base of a building, part of which is below the ground

FRESCO: designs painted directly on walls or ceilings

LEGEND: a story coming from the past

PORTICO: porch or covered outside hallway

PRESERVE: to keep in good condition without change

PRESIDIO: a settlement of military men

QUADRANGLE: four-sided shape; the shape of most missions

RANCHOS: large ranches often many miles from mission proper where crops were grown and animal herds grazed

REBUILD: to build again; to repair a great deal of something

REPLICA: a close copy of the original

REREDOS: the wall behind the main altar inside the church

*RESTORATION: to bring something back to its original condition (see * below)

SANCTUARY: area inside, at the front of the church where the main altar is found

SECULARIZATION: something not religious; a law in mission days taking the mission buildings away from the church and placing them under government rule

*ORIGINAL: the first one; the first one built

BIBLIOGRAPHY

Bauer, Helen. *California Mission Days.* Sacramento, CA: Calfiornia State Department of Education, 1957.

Engbeck, Joseph H., Jr. *La Purísima Mission.* Sacramento, CA: California Resources Agency, Department of Parks and Recreation, no date.

Goodman, Marian. *Missions of California.* Redwood City, CA: Redwood City Tribune, 1962.

Sunset Editors. *The California Missions.* Menlo Park, CA: Lane Publishing Company, 1979.

Wright, Ralph B., ed. *California Missions.* Arroyo Grande, CA 93420: Hubert A. Lowman, 1977.

For more information about this mission, write to:

La Purísima Mission
State Historic Park
RFD 102
Lompoc, CA 93436

It is best to enclose a self-addressed, stamped envelope and a small amount of money to pay for brochures and pictures the mission might send you.

Credits:
Cover art and Father Serra Illustration: Ellen Grim
Illustrations: Alfredo de Batuc
Ground Layout: Mary Boulé
Printing: Print NW, Tacoma, Washington 98499